*Whispers of Hope*

© 2013 Christian Art Gifts, RSA
          Christian Art Gifts Inc., IL, USA

Second edition 2017

Designed by Christian Art Gifts

Images used under license from Shutterstock.com

Printed in China

ISBN 978-1-4321-2558-5

17  18  19  20  21  22  23  24  25  26  –  10  9  8  7  6  5  4  3  2  1